Dilawar Karadaghi
MY COUNTRY'S HAIR TURNED WHITE
SELECTED POEMS

Edited by Jiyar Homer

Translated from the Kurdish by
Jiyar Homer and Mike Baynham

Introduced by Mike Baynham
with notes by the poet

PUBLICATIONS
2024

Published by Arc Publications,
Nanholme Mill, Shaw Wood Road
Todmorden OL14 6DA, UK
www.arcpublications.co.uk

978 1911469-74-2

Design by Tony Ward
Printed in the UK by TJ Books,
Padstow, Cornwall

Cover painting © Jaza Bakr,
by kind premission of the artist.

ACKNOWLEDGEMENTS
The publisher wishes to acknowledge the American University of
Iraq, Sulaimani (AUIS), and Kashkul,
its Center for Arts & Culture, for providing the support
for Jiyar Homer to engage in this project with Mike Baynham.

Arc Chapbook Series
Series Editor: Tony Ward

CONTENTS

Introduction: / 5

Dilawar Karadaghi started writing poetry in 1982 when he was 19 years old. He is a key member of what has become known as the Post-Revolution Generation, named after the revolution of 1991 which defeated and expelled Iraqi forces from Kurdistan after the battle of Kirkuk. This triggered an economic, social and cultural flowering to which Dilawar has contributed. This is how the poet describes the significance of this moment:

> Actually, Kurdish poetry set foot into a new and different era after the 1991 revolution. The revolution created a different atmosphere for Kurdish literature than that of the eighties. It opened a new way of expression for a new generation of poets, one of whom I am proud to say was myself. The beginning of the seventies and post March 11, Kurdish poetry and literature saw a similar flowering but its outcomes in terms of characteristics are different than those post-revolution. [Dilawar Karadaghi, personal communication].

Yet, while crucially located in the Kurdish situation, Dilawar's poetry is intimately engaged with current international poetic trends and the role of translation into Kurdish is crucial in this. The poet describes the formative part his reading of iconic modernist work in Arabic, Persian, Turkish and a range of European languages played in his emergence as a poet:

> My journey into poetry began with the heritage of Classical Kurdish literature, especially Nali and Mahwi. Then, I explored the works of contemporary Kurdish poets like Abdulla Goran and Sherko Bekas, and delved into translated Arabic, Persian, Turkish... including Badr Shakir al-Sayyab, Adonis, Mahmoud Darwish, Forough Farrokhzad, Ahmad Shamloo, Nazim Hikmet, and in Western literature, Federico García Lorca, Pablo Neruda, Paul Éluard, Louis Aragon, among others.
>
> During that phase, I read whatever I could find, due to the lack of sources of world literature in Kurdish. Of course, I didn't intend or plan for those readings to turn me into a poet. The desire to become a poet emerged later, as my worldview on existence, human beings, and existential issues took shape. This desire grew as I gradually left my city and started

reading in Arabic and then Persian, opening up new horizons for looking and thinking. Without realising it, the desire to be a poet awakened within me. [Dilawar Karadaghi, personal communication]

While translated works significantly influenced his emergence as a poet, Dilawar has himself made a significant contribution to literary translation into Kurdish, a fact that is important for our understanding of the local / global positioning of his poetry. He speaks Kurdish, Swedish, Arabic and Persian, as well as some English. He has translated works of more than thirty writers, including Friedrich Hölderlin, Nikos Kazantzakis, Hjalmar Söderberg, Ingmar Bergman, André Malraux, Stig Dagerman, Theodor Kallifatides, Bohumil Hrabal, Anton Chekhov and Françoise Sagan. His work consists of more than sixty books. His most recent published works include a translation of Andrei Tarkovsky's diary, *Martyrology* (published by Faber as *Time Within Time*) and a selection of thirty world poets into Kurdish. He is now living in the city of Slemani, Kurdistan Region.

Leading critics have praised his work: the great Kurdish poet Sherko Bekas has spoken in interviews about the importance of Dilawar Karadaghi, describing him as a new voice in Kurdish literature. The iconic Kurdish writer, Bachtyar Ali, says of Dilawar, remarking on the clarity of his poetic expression, "Dilawar's poetic voice is one of the clearest… his words have a strange clarity in their dimension… they carry a tenderness and clarity which is rarely seen…" His poem 'A Child Who Returned From There Told Us', was translated into English by the Kurdish poet and translator Choman Hardi, and has been added to the education curriculum in Australia. The famous Polish-Jewish-American architect, Daniel Libeskind, borrowed the idea for building a Kurdistan museum in Hawler from a poem by Karadaghi. The American poet and translator Alana Marie Levinson-LaBrosse describes a meeting with him thus:

When, one day, I had the honour to sit down one afternoon with Dilawar Karadaghi, I was struck by the quiet that seemed to hang in the air around him. The lobby of the Slemani Palace Hotel echoed with the hum and honking of afternoon bazaar traffic, but he himself sat still, composed, peaceful. It wasn't until years later that I would see more fully how hard Dilawar had worked to achieve and maintain this peace – for peace is not self-sustaining, especially not for a Kurd. [Levinson-LaBrosse, *Introduction to Dilawar Karadaghi's Collected Poetry from 1992–2020*]

Dilawar's poetry is characterised by the long years of persecution, marginalisation and struggle that have marked the Kurdish experience, most explicitly in this selection in the poem 'Autumn of the Kurds'. Many writers have commented on the distinctiveness of Dilawar's poetic voice. Bachtyar Ali, echoing Levinson-LaBrosse's observation, points to a despair and melancholy which never turns to anger, being in a sense held by the poem, perhaps echoing the poetic positioning of Mahmoud Darwish:

> There is a despair in Dilawar's poetry that will never turn into anger, this is the difference between Dilawar's poetry and most of our other poets. For instance, when we talk about despair, at some point, all the longing and despair becomes a fierce anger. That is, in some way, it becomes a violent language. Even in my own literary experience there is always a moment of longing, of not-reaching and despair which turns into a fierce confrontation with the world. In Dilawar's poems, this turn to anger just does not exist. [Bachtyar Ali]

And yet this restraint can make the irruptions of violence and pain where they do occur even more powerful. In the poem 'Poets' Neighbourhood', an idyllic childhood is evoked, only to be shattered towards the end of the poem when the reader is confronted by the abduction and murder of a childhood friend Yousf, who returns at night to beg his mother to bury his body. The shock here is somehow evocative of a similar shock in Rimbaud's 'Le Dormeur du Val'.

As we have seen, Dilawar's poetry exists at the interface between the distinctive history and experience of the Kurds and international poetic trends, nowhere more than in his focus on displacement and mobility, which indexes both the history of displacement and diaspora of the Kurdish people and a worldwide focus in contemporary literature on *dépaysement* and mobility. Again Bachtyar Ali eloquently puts his finger on this characteristic:

> In Dilawar's poetry, there is always a traveller who does not reach their destination. There is a person who travels in all of his poems. This situation is repeated in many forms and

in many metaphors and in many secret stories in the poems. Some person of whom we have no idea of where he travels from nor any idea of where he is going. That is to say, it has the conditions of a permanent journey, whose beginning or end is not clear. From my point of view, often the novel as a genre can handle this kind of situation. I mean, the situation of the eternal traveller who can be a metaphorical image or symbol of the whole situation of modern human beings, or for the whole situation of Kurdish human beings, which is to be a traveller in a state of permanent mobility, never stopping and never reaching their destination. This state is deeply reflected in Dilawar's poetry. I am not able to determine whether it is a conscious reflection or a subconscious experience, but in his poetry I always see a traveller who is travelling in a thin mist and not reaching their destination. [Bachtyar Ali]

So virtually every poem collected here contains a variation in some shape or form on the theme of leaving. This is echoed in the short introductory notes provided by the poet for each poem. Fatima, in 'Fatima's Night Out', is leaving, and plans never to return, on the run from her pain. In the 'Poets' Neighbourhood', Yousf is taken, leaving involuntarily, while the poet chooses to leave, to get out in time. In 'Autumn of the Kurds', the theme of leaving is condensed into the image of two friends saying goodbye at a bus station – the Kurdish bus station – indexing the iconic status of leaving for the Kurdish experience, again here with an echo of Darwish:

In the Kurdish bus terminal
when my friend said goodbye
I brought my mouth close to his ear and
whispered, "You won't see me again so soon,
forgive me… Oh my lonely friend
goodbye

In 'Oppression', a group of friends pose for a photograph, a photograph that is predicated on the melancholy of separation:

Take a photograph of us
a group picture in black and white
Perhaps
we'll not see each other again

'That Village' might seem to be the exception to the theme of leaving that is threaded so powerfully through the poems, and yet even here the poem, while celebrating the dynamics of settlement, is full of intimations of leaving: the flight of birds, the passing clouds, even the sun in its daily trajectory from East to West, the weather itself, the whirlwind and the migratory breezes that commit suicide in the moonlight's arms. In the last poem 'In the Blink of an Eye, My Country's Hair Turned White', from which the title of this chapbook is taken, there is a hallucinatory horror of leaving, when what leaves is the everyday coordinates of reality, the seasons of the year, the hours in a day, and one senses the poet struggling with the limits of language and its capacity to mean, in order to convey an atrocity that is barely held by the poem.

A final word on the translation process. As a translator of poetry, my comfort zone is Spanish and Arabic and, to a much lesser extent, Persian. Kurdish is a closed book to me, though I can read the script, so in this translation process I worked with Jiyar Homer, an experienced and prolific translator from Kurdish into Spanish and English, dedicated to making Kurdish literature available through translation. Jiyar provided his poetical rendering into English which was our starting point. So with Jiyar in Slemani and me in Yorkshire, we worked together via GoogleDoc, often in real time, to refine and polish the translation. We are, therefore, not talking about a conventional stereotypical "bridge translation" relationship, such has been recently critiqued by Calleja & Collins in *Asymptote* (Calleja & Collins, 2024): Jiyar brought to the table his poetic translation and our collaboration lay in working through and finalising that translation. Our relative contributions to the translation process are reflected in the order of the credits.

It has been a privilege to work with Jiyar Homer on this project, but in writing the introduction, aspiring, as Walter Benjamin did, to a text which is a tapestry of quotations, I have also relied on the perspectives of poets and translators who can comment insightfully on the qualities of Dilawar's poetry through long and first-hand experience: poets Sherko Bekas and Bachtyar Ali, the poet and translator Alana Marie Levinson-LaBrosse and indeed the words of the poet himself who has generously engaged with us to explicate his work as well as providing an explanatory note for each poem. To all of these we would like to extend our heartfelt thanks.

Mike Baynham

ئێوارەی فادیمە

گەنجی و کچێتی فادیمە بە باسی پاکیزەیی و داوێنپاکیی بە تاڵان چوون. فادیمە گەیشتووەتە تەنی، ئێوارە دەچێتە دەرەوە، بەڵام نیازی گەڕانەوەی نییە. برینەکانی، یادەوەری و ئازار و بکوژەکانی لەگەڵ خۆیدا دەبات. ئەو حەز دەکات عاشق ببێت، دەڵێت عاشقان هەمیشە لە سەفەردان. فادیمە نازانێت سەفەر چییە، ئەو ئاشنایە بە ڕاکردن و سەرهەڵگرتن، ڕاکردن لە کچێنییە کوژراوەکەی، سەرهەڵگرتن لە مێژووە خوێناوییەکەی.

من ئەوم
ئەم ئێوارەیە سەفەرم هەیە
بە ڕوخسەتی ئێوە
ئەم ئێوارەیە، من دەچمە سەما
بیرم ناچێ بلوسە پرتەقاڵییەکەم بپۆشم
بیرم ناچێ چاوانم بڕێژم بە هەتاو
بیرم ناچێ دوو گوارە لە گوێم بکەم بە ڕەنگی کچێنیی
بیرم ناچێ بە گاڵتەوە خۆم لە چۆلەکە خەواڵووەکان
توورە بکەم و بڵێم:
کچینە دەی چیتان کرد با بڕۆین،
گورج کەن!

من ئەوم... ئەوێک کە بیری ناچێ
ئەم ئێوارەیە لە سەفەردایە و
دەشزانێ کە مرۆڤ لە سەفەردا بوو.. دەبێ
وەک بەرد بێدەنگیی بەڵەد بێ
دەبێ هێند بە مشمور و وریا بێ
کە چۆن بە دریژایی ڕێگە لە خاڵی بنۆڕێ
دەبێ بزانێ لە کوێدا وچانێک دەدا و
لە کوێدا نوکتەیەک دەگێڕێتەوە و
لە کوێدا عەشق دەکا و
لە کوێدا خۆی دەکوژێ و
لە کوێدا دەکوژرێ و
لە کوێدا لەبەرخۆیەوە دەڵێ: ئۆف... خودایە
چەند بێ تاقەت و شەکەت و تەنیام!

من ئەوم و
دڵنیام کە تەنها عاشقان دەچنە سەفەر
ئەوەی عاشق نەبێ ئەو لە کوێ و

10

FATIMA'S EVENING OUT

Fatima is a woman whose youth and girlhood were wasted in talks of virginity and chastity. She is done; she has had enough. She is leaving for an evening out, but she has no intention of returning. She carries her wounds, her memories, her pains and her murderers on a lifelong journey. She wishes she was in love. She says only those in love are always travelling. Fatima has no idea what travel is; she is familiar with running away from her past, from memories of her murdered virginity, and her bloody history.

I'm her
the one who's leaving this evening.
With your permission of course,
this evening, I'm going out dancing.
I won't forget to wear my orange blouse
I won't forget to paint my eyelids with the sunlight
I won't forget to wear earrings the colour of virginity
I won't forget to play angry
with the sleepy sparrows and say,
"Girls! Where are you?
Get a move on! Let's go!"

I'm her... who doesn't forget
who is going out this evening and
who also knows that when you are out
you must know how to be silent as a stone
how to be ever so careful and attentive
how to fix your gaze on a certain point
where to take a break and
where to tell a joke and
where to make love and
where does suicide fit in and
where to get killed and
where to mutter, "Oh... God,
How miserable, how tired and lonely I am!"

I am her and
I'm sure that only lovers leave on a journey
if they are not in love
what has it to do with flying?

فڕین له کوێ؟
تەنها عاشقانن که بەتەما نین کەس
له دوا وێستگە چاوەڕیان بکا
تەنها عاشقانن که هەمیشه له سەفەردا
نەختێ ئاسمانیان پێیه بۆ موفەرک
ئەوان لەوەتەی هەن
دوو مالیان هەبووه... مالێک له بیابان و
ئەوی دیشیان له تەنیشت باران
بمبوورە که بەم هەموو برینەوه ماتلم کردی
بەم هەموو ژانەوه و بەم هەموو خوێنەوه
که قولپ قولپ دەڕوا له کچێنی
له شەوی بکوژان
له مێژوو
به ڕادیەک ئێشم زۆره که گەرەکمه
هێند توند بزریکێنم
هەموو ئەم ولاته ساردەتان بهێنمه سەیر
هەموو ئەم عالەمه سارده
دوو باغی وەک خۆم خوێناوی دێنه ژێر بالم
هێند دلم پڕه که نازانم بۆ مردن دەچم
یاخود دەمەوێ هەر بدوێم و شت بگێرمەوه و
تا بەیانی هەر خۆش نەکەمەوه و ببارم

من ئەوم
ئەوێ که ئیدی له چارەی نووسرا
دەبێ تا ماوه لەسەفەردا بێ
دەبێ تا ماوه لەوودیو پەنجەرەوه و لەژێر باراندا،
سلاو بکا لەو ژنانەی که به غەمباری له دایک بوون و
به غەمباری مردن
سلاو بکا
لەو ژنانەی لەوەتەی هەن قژ دەڕننەوه
لەوەتەی هەن به ژانەوەن
لەوەتەی هەن سەر دەبردرێن و هەتک دەکرێن و
لەوەتەی هەن لێوانلێون له تووڕەیی
له زریکه
له چاوەڕوانی و تەقەی دەرگا

من ئەوم
ئەویک که ئیدی له چارەی نووسرا
دەبێ ببێته هاوڕێی گیانیبەگیانی ئەو ژنانەی

Only lovers who don't desire anyone
wait for them at the last stop
only lovers who are always on a journey
have a little sky as a blessing
have had two homes ever since they existed…
one in the desert and
the other alongside the rain
I'm sorry to keep you waiting with all these wounds
with all this pain and all this blood
which bubbles out from virginity
from the night of murderers
from the history
I have so much pain that I want to scream out
to bring all this cold country to see you
all this cold world
two bloody gardens just like me nestle in my arms
I'm so heart-stricken that I don't even know
if I'm going to die or if I want to keep talking and telling stories
or if I will rain without stopping until tomorrow

I am her
who is destined
to journey till her last breath
who beyond the window and beneath the rain,
has to greet women born in sorrow
who died in sorrow
until her last breath
to greet
the women who have been pulling out their hair ever since
they existed
who have been in pain ever since they existed
who have been beheaded and raped ever since they existed
who have been brimful of anger
of screaming
of waiting and knocks at the door

I'm her
the one who is destined
to become a soulmate of these women
whose eyes are full of murdered seas

که چاوانیان پڕە لە زەریای کوژراو
که گوێیان پڕە لە چڕەی خنکاو
که گەرووویان پڕە لە کۆتری گریاو
که دڵیان پڕە لە نامەی تەرە کراو

من ئەوم
عاشقێ که ئیدی هەتا ماوم
هەمیشه لە سەفەردام!

گەرەکی شاعیران

سەفەر، بەدەم خەوەوە ڕۆیشتن، دیارنەمان، هەموو جۆرەکانی جێهێشتن تێمای دووبارەی ناو شیعرەکانی قەرەداغین. گەرەکی شاعیران به ڕۆژێکی هەتاو و به ڕووالەت شاد دەست پێ دەکات. هەر زوو وێنەی ئارامی و سەقامگیری به دەرکەوتنی شوێنێنی شوێنێنی دردۆنگ و وەسوەسەی ڕۆیشتن تێک دەشکێت. چونکه ئەگەر نەڕوێت، ئەوا دەبردرێت، وەک یوسف، به بێ ویستی خۆت.

دونیا هەتاوه
بەر پەنجەرەکەم سێبەر
تەیرێ لەبەر هەتاوەکەدا،
هەڵنیشتوو به جلکی ڕەشەوە لەسەر چڵی بەفر
خەواڵوو دەچمە بەر پەنجەرەکه
دایکم لە هەیوان به دیار قوڵپی سەماوەرەوە
دیژڵەمه دەخواتەوە و لەبەرخۆیەوە قسان دەکا
بەو بەیانییه
زولێخا لە سەربان جلک هەڵدەخا

ڕیزێک جێگاپێی تازه،
ڕۆیشتوو تا بەردەرگای حەوشه
هی کەسێ که لە خەونیدا چووه بۆ شوێنێ
بیردەکەمەوه ڕەنگبێ جێگاپێی خاوەن ماڵەکەی
سەرەوەمان بێ
که شەوێکی درەنگ جانتای پێچاوەتەوه و
چووه بۆ سەفەرێکی دوور
یان ڕەنگه تەنها بۆ پیاسەیەکی کورت چووبێ بۆ کۆڵان
خۆ دەشبێ جێگاپێی خۆم بن
که ئێستا به نیازم بچم بۆ جێگایەکی تر!

14

whose ears are full of drowned whispers
whose throats are full of weeping pigeons
whose hearts are full of driven away letters

I'm her
a lover who will always be on a journey
until my last breath!

POETS' NEIGHBOURHOOD

Travelling, sleepwalking, disappearing, all forms of leaving are repeated themes in Karadaghi's poems. The poem starts with a sunny day in a seemingly happy home in an idealised neighbourhood. The image of stability is shattered when footprints appear, murmuring a need to leave. Because if you don't leave, you will be taken like Yousf, against your will.

Everywhere is sunny
my window is in shadow
a bird alights on a snow branch
dressing in black the sunlight.
Sleepily I go to the window
my mother drinks tea without sugar and murmurs
in the corridor while the samovar bubbles
in that early morning

Zulaikha hangs clothes on the rooftop
a new row of footprints
walked up to the threshold is left by
someone who has sleep walked to somewhere else
I think perhaps they are the footprints
of the landlord who lives upstairs
who packed his bags at midnight
and went on a long journey
or perhaps he went for a short stroll
around the alley
It's even possible they are my footprints
and that currently I intend to go somewhere else!

دونیا هەتاوە
حەزم لە خواردنەوەی چایەکی زۆر شیرینە
پاشان جانتا بێچمەوە و لە دوای ماشێنێکدا دانیشم
هەست دەکەم... دڵم خەراپ خۆشە
لەبەرخۆمەوە دوعا دەکەم
خودایە ئەمە وابێ!
من لەم ماڵەدا کوڕێکی بەختەوەر بووم
خۆش بوون ئەو خەوانەی کە لەم ماڵەدا بینیمن
میهرەبان بوو ئەو هەتاوەی
کە بە چەپک خۆی دەکرد بە ژووردا
ناشبێ نەزاکەتی ئەو مەلانەم بیربچێ
کە دەیانزانی شاعیرم و
کاتێ دەهاتمەوە ماڵەوە و خۆم بە حەوشەدا دەکرد
بە ئەدەبەوە دەیانجریواند!

من لەم گەرەکەدا دراوسێی باشم هەبوون
دراوسێی میهرەبان
بە دەگمەن ... دەنا هەر هەموو
سەریان لە شیعر... بە تایبەتی لە شیعری ناڵی دەخوورا
منالەکانیان بە دەگمەن .. دەنا هەر هەموو
دەفتەرەکانیان پڕ بوو لە دە لە دە و
زۆر باشە .. ئافەرین!
با ئەوەش بڵێم
کە هەر لەم گەرەکەدا هاوڕێیەکم هەبوو
ناوی یوسف بوو
گەرچی لە هیچی کەم نەبوو
بەڵام تەنیا بوو وەک گوڵدان
ئەو، جگە لەوەی شاعیرێکی باش بوو
جاروبار نیگاری دەکێشا و خەتیشی تا بڵێی خۆش بوو
پاییزێکی درەنگ
ئەو کوڕە تاقانەیان ڕفاند و
چوون لە جێگایەکی دوور کوشتیان و بەجێیانهێشت
ئێوارەیەک یوسف بە کوژراوی و بەپێی خۆی
خۆی کردەوە بە ماڵدا و بە گریانەوە گوتی:
وای دایکە ... ئازارم زۆرە
بمنێژن!

Everywhere is sunny
I would like to sip a very sweet cup of tea
then pack my bags and sit in the back of a car
I feel… that I'm unhappily happy
I am muttering prayers,
"Oh God, let this be real!"
I was a happy boy in this house
they were joyful the dreams in this house
kind was the sun
that entered in a handful of flowers
I should not forget the gentle manners of the birds
who knew I was a poet and
when I returned home and entered the courtyard
would sing politely!

I had good neighbours in this neighbourhood
kind neighbours
everyone with the rare exception
enjoyed poetry… especially the poetry of Nali
the children too… with the rare exception
the marks in their notebooks were all 10/10,
excellents and well-dones!
I should add that
I had a friend in the neighbourhood
his name was Yousf
although he did not lack for anything
he was lonely like a flower-pot
he was not just a good poet,
he drew sketches from time to time
and had very nice handwriting
one late autumn
they snatched that irreplaceable boy and
killed him in a far away place and left him alone.
One evening, Yousf, dead and on his feet
entered home and said, sobbing,
"Oh, mother…
I feel so much pain,
bury me!"

دونیا هەتاوە
دلم خەراپ خۆشە
حەز دەکەم بەر لەوەی جانتاکەم هەلگرم و
خواحافیزی بکەم و بڕۆم،
خەونەکەی دوێنێ شەوم بۆ دایکم بگێڕمەوە
بەلام نا... بێ سوودە
دایکم هەمیشە پێی وایە
کە من هەر لە مندالییەوە
زۆر شەوان جانتام پێچاوەتەوە و
بەدەم خەوەوە ڕۆیشتووم!

گۆتینبۆرگ شوباتی ٢٠١٠

پاییزی کوردەکان

دوو کەسایەتی، یەکێکیان ستڕانبێژ و ئەویدی جەنگاوەر، یەکیان نەغمە و ئەویدییان
نەعرەتە، دوو هێل؛ دوو ڕیتمی لێکدی جیاواز بەلام هاوسەفەر و هاوچارەنووس.
هێلێک؛ جێببێکی خۆلاوی و ئێوارەی شەقامێکی پڕ هەراوزەنا و هوتافکێشان و
قەرەبالخی. هێلێکی تر بیدەنگی و چۆلەوانییەک کە سیخناخە بە خەم و دردۆنگییەکی
کوردی. دوو هێلی هارمۆنیک لە شێوەی خەمگینترین ستڕاندا دڕێژ دەبنەوە.

دۆست نامە دەنووسێ
ئەم ئێوارەیە وەرە بۆ جادەی کوردەکان
پەلەپەل خۆم دەگەیەنمە ئەوێ
هەر یەکەمان بە ڕۆژنامەیەکی لوولکراوەوە
لەبنهەنگلدا
لارەمل بەو جادە غەمگینەدا
بەرەو خوار دەبینەوە
زوو زووش دەست بۆ دلمان دەبەین
تا دلنیابین کە ئاخۆ شتێکمان
لە شوێنێ لێ نەکەوتووە
دۆست دەلێ: با بگەڕێینەوە... وا بزانم
سەروو لەتێ لە دلمان
لە دوکانەکەی سەرەوە
لەناو ئینجانەکانی کچە گولفرۆشەکەدا
لەبیر چووە!

18

Everywhere is sunny
I'm unhappily happy
before picking up my bag,
saying farewell and leaving,
I would like tell my mother
last night's dream
but no… it's pointless
my mother always thinks
that ever since childhood
night after night I have packed my bag
and sleep walked away!

Gothenburg, February, 2010

AUTUMN OF THE KURDS

Two characters; one a singer, the other a warrior; one melodious, the other a roar. Two lines, two different rhythms, yet the same destination and the same fate. One line, a dusty Jeep driving through a crowded evening of chanting protestors; another line a silence brimming with Kurdish sorrow and doubt. Two lines that extend harmoniously in the manner of the saddest song.

My friend messaged me,
"Come to Kurdish Street this evening"
I got there in a hurry
each of us with a rolled newspaper
under our arms
necks bent we're going down
that sad street
we often touch our hearts
to make sure something hasn't dropped off
us anywhere
my friend said, "Let's go back… I think
each one of us left
a piece of our heart
in the shop above
in the flower-pots of the girl selling flowers!"

دۆست بەدەم پیاسەوە بە جادەی کوردەکانا
دەڵێ: ئادەی گوێچکەت بێنە
با شتێکت پێبڵێم
خەیال دەمباتەوە و دەڵێم: ئادەی
دۆست بە چ‌پە ئەڵێ:
پێتچۆنە هەردووکمان سبەینێ لە غەزەتەدا
بانگەوازێک بکەین
کە سەروو لەتێک لە دڵمان دەبە خشین
دەڵێم: ئاخر بە کێ؟
دۆست دەڵێ: من دەیبەخشمە بالندەیەکی دڵپێکراو
تۆیش
لەم جادە قەرەباڵخ و غەمگین و بەرینەی
کوردەکاندا
بیدەرە کوردێکی دڵشکاو!
لە جادەی کوردەکاندا
لەو هەموو هەراهەرا و هۆڕن و
هات و هاوارەدا
جیێیکی بێدەنگ و بریندار و خۆڵاوی
سەرنجمان رادەکێشێ
نەفەرەکەی لای شۆفێرەکەوە
جامەکەی لای خۆی تا نیوە دەکا تەوە و
بە دەستێکی دڵشکاو سڵاوێکمان لێدەکا
دۆست بە زەردەخەنەیەکەوە دەڵێ
دەزانی ئەو پیاوە کێ بوو؟
من دەڵێم:
وا بزانم... کاک ئیسماعیل خانی شکاک بوو
دۆست دەڵێ: نا ...
دەڵێم: باشە کێ بوو؟
دۆست دەڵێ: دەبوو بە دەستە غەمگینەکەی و
هاڕەی شکانی دڵیدا
بتزانیبا
ئەو پیاوە
سەی عەلی ئەسغەری کوردستانیی بوو
لە دووڕیانی خوار جادەی کوردەکاندا
لە سینگی هەریەک لە من و دۆستدا
لەتێ دڵ لێ دەدا و
بانگمان دەکا
لەتێ بانگمان دەکا بچینەوە بۆ دارستان
بۆ لای باپیرە و داپیرە دڵشکاوەکانمان
لەتێکیش بۆ شارانێکی دوور
بۆ لای لەتە شکاوەکەی تری دڵی خۆمان!

20

My friend was strolling down Kurdish Street
he said, "Come on, bring your ears close,
let me tell you something."
Imagination gripped me and I said, "Let's hear it!"
My friend whispered,
"How about we both declare
in the newspaper tomorrow
that we are donating a piece of our hearts."
"But who to?", I said
"I'll donate it to a bird shot in the heart,
and you
on this crowded, wide, sad Kurdish street
grant it to a heart-broken Kurd!" said my friend.
On Kurdish Street
among all the noise, horns and clamour
a quiet, wounded, dusty Jeep
caught our attention
the passenger next to the driver
half opened his window and
greeted us with a heart-broken hand
"Do you know who that man was?"
My friend said with a smile,
"I think it's… Mr. Simko Shikak," I said
"No…" my friend said
"Well, who was it?" I said
"You should have known"
my friend said,
"by his sad hands and
the clank of his heart breaking
that man was
Sayyid Ali Asghar Kurdistani."
At the intersection down from Kurdish Street
in the chest of both me and my friend
a piece of heart beats
and is calling us
a piece calls us to go back to the forest
to our heartbroken grandparents
and another piece to distant cities
to the other broken piece of our hearts!

له گەراجی کوردەکان
که دۆست خواحافیزییم لێدەکا
دەم له گوێچکەی نزیک دەکەمەوە و
بەچپە پێی دەڵێم: ئیتر وا زوو نامبینیتەوە
ببوورە... ئەی دۆستی تەنیا
به دوعا
من ئیتر له ماڵ نایەمه دەرێ
ئەوه نەبێ که جار جار دێمه بانیژەکەم
یان گوێ هەڵدەخەم بۆ لوورەی هاتنی ئەمبۆلانس
یاخود چاو دەگێرم به ئاسماندا
بۆ دەرکەوتنی فڕۆکەیەک
که لەم پاییزه پەتییه کوردییەم هەڵگرێ و
بۆ پاییزێکی ترم با!

که له گەراجی کوردەکان
خواحافیزی له یەک دەکەین
له جامی نیوه دادراوه ی پاسەکەوە
دۆست به کوردییەکی دڵشکاو
پێمدەڵێ:
من ئیتر بۆ پاییزێکی تر دەچمەوە
به دوو سێ کتێب
سێ چوار ژماره تەلەفۆن
چوار پێنج وێنەی ڕەش و سپیی و
تاقه ئەدرێسی غەمگینی
ماڵه غەریبەکەی دڵتەوه!

سلێمانی یونی ٢٠١١

غەدر

قەرەباڵغییەکی پر له چۆڵەوانی لەم شیعرەدا ئامادەیه. هەرچەند داوای گرتنی
وێنەیەکی به کۆمەڵه که تیایدا گەرەکی پر له مندال و دایک و باوەش و ڕوانین
و ئازار و فرمێسک دەرکەوێت، بەڵام ناتوانیت ئەو زەریایه له چۆڵەوانی نەبینیت
کاتێک وشەگەلی «بیابان» و «تەنیایی» و «ڕاگوێزان» و «تەرم» دەبینیت.
هەرچەنده وێنەیەکی بەکۆمەڵه، بەڵام وێنەی تەنیاییشه. هەرچەند پێکەوەین، بەڵام
به تەنیا ئەزموونی غەدر دەکەین.

22

In the Kurdish bus terminal
when my friend said goodbye
I brought my mouth close to his ear and
whispered, "You won't see me again so soon,
forgive me... Oh my lonely friend
goodbye
I won't leave home anymore
except to step out onto my balcony from time to time
or listen to the howls of an ambulance
or look around at the sky
for a plane to appear
that can carry me from this pure Kurdish autumn
and take me to another autumn!"

When we said goodbye to each other
in the Kurdish bus terminal
through the bus's half-open window
my friend told me
in heart-broken Kurdish,
"I'm going back for another autumn
with two or three books
three or four phone numbers
four or five black-and-white photographs
and the only sad address
of your heart's strange house!"

Slemani, June, 2011

OPPRESSION

A fullness filled with emptiness is evoked in this poem. Although it starts with a request for a group picture to be taken that will show a neighbourhood full of kids, mothers, hugs, gazes, pains and tears, the reader can't help but see the sea of emptiness when 'desert', 'loneliness', 'displacement' and 'corpses' are mentioned. Although it is a group picture, it is also a picture of solitude. Although together, yet alone, the picture is taken. Although together, yet alone, we live our lives in the face of oppression.

بۆ هونەرمەند سیروان رەئووف

وێنەیەکمان بگرە
وێنەیەکی رەش و سپی بە کۆمەڵ
دەشێ
یەکتر نەبینینەوە ئیتر
وێنەیەک
کە پشتمان لە چۆڵەوانی و
کە ئەوبەرمان تەنیایی و
کە غەمبار
لەناو چیمەنی باراندا
راوەستابین و
دەستمان نابێتە سەر شانی
یەکتر!
وێنەیەکی بەکۆمەڵمان بگرە

وێنەیەک
کە تیایدا
ئەو رێگەیە ژەهرڕێژ کرابێ
کە شەوانە هەتاو
ترێی پێدا دەنێرێتەوە شار و
کە هەنگ
کۆمە کۆم
لێیەوە شیلە دەباتەوە
ماڵی قسە و
کە مانگ،
چۆر چۆر لێیەوە
قردێلەی تریفە بە دیاری
دەپەرێنێتەوە بۆ کەزی و پرچی
کچە شەرمنەکانی خۆی!
لەم دەربەندەوە
عەتر ئاودیو نابێ
چ جای سڵاو
با ناتوانی بەم بنارەدا هەڵزنی
چ جای نامە
دەستتم بدەرێ
وێنەیەکی بەکۆمەڵمان بگرە
دەستتم بدەرێ
تا وەک ئێوارانی گەڕانەوەی غەدر
لەژێر هەرەسی تەنیایی خۆماندا
نغرۆ نەبووین

24

for artist Sirwan Rauf

Take a picture of us
a group picture in black-and-white
perhaps
we'll not see each other again
a picture
with our backs to desert
facing towards loneliness and
standing
sadly
in a teeming lawn of rain
with our hands on
each other's shoulders!
Take a group picture of us

A picture
in which
that road has been poisoned
and the sunlight at night
sends grapes back to the city
so that the hunchbacked bee
can take nectar from it
to the house of speech
so that the moon,
taking it drop by drop
can hand the hair ribbon
as a gift
to the tresses
of his shy girls!
From this valley
perfume cannot cross
let alone a greeting
the wind cannot climb this foothill
let alone a letter
give me your hands
take a group picture of us
before when we aren't lost to each other
like the rainy nights of flight
drop by drop
give me your hands
before when we haven't sunk

دەستتم بدەرێ
وێنەیەکمان بگرە رەش و سپیی
وێنەیەک،
که بە کۆمەڵ ... بە تەنیا
دەکوژرێین
وێنەیەک
که بە کۆمەڵ ... بە تەنیا
رادەگوێزرێین
وێنەیەک
که بە تەماشای کوژرانی یەکتر
راودەنرێین
وێنەیەک
که بە کۆمەڵ ... بە تەنیا
بۆ ناشتنی تەرمی یەکتر
هەڵدەکەنرێین
دەستتم بدەرێ
هەستەوە
بە فلاشی باڵ لەیەکدانی
کۆترێ
وێنەیەکی بەکۆمەڵمان بگرە
وێنەیەک
که بە کۆمەڵ ئابڵوقه دراوین
به چەقۆ
پەپوولەشمان لێ دیار نییه
چ جای خودا
وێنەیەک
که بەکۆمەڵ گەمارۆ دراوین
به کەڵبه
دەرگایەکمان لێ دیار نییه
چ جای زەریا
هەستەوە
بە فلاشی رەشداگەرانی خەونێ
وێنەیەکی بە کۆمەڵمان بگرە
وێنەیەک
پڕ پڕ بێ له دایک
پڕ پڕ بێ له کزەی جەرگ
وێنەیەک
پڕ پڕ بێ له داماویی

like the evenings of the oppression's return
under the avalanche of our loneliness
give me your hands
take a picture of us in black-and-white
a picture
in which we get killed
together... alone
a picture
in which we get displaced
together... alone
a picture
in which we get pursued
to watch each other being killed
together... alone
a picture
in which we are dug up
to bury each other's corpses
together... alone
give me your hands
get up again
with the wings' flash
of a pigeon
take a group picture of us
a picture
in which we are all under siege
with knives
where we can't see butterflies either
let alone God
a picture
in which we are all encircled
with fangs
where we can't see a door
let alone the sea
get up again
with a flash of a dream that turns black
take a group picture of us
a picture
full of mothers
of heartache
a picture
full of desperation

پڕ پڕ بێ لە کۆست
پڕ پڕ بێ لە منااڵنی گەڕەک
وێنەیەک
پڕ پڕ بێ لە گڵەیی
پڕ پڕ بێ لە ژان
وێنەیەک
پڕ پڕ بێ لە باوەش
پڕ پڕ بێ لە هەڵدێران
پڕ پڕ بێ لە ماچ و مووچ و
پڕ پڕ بێ لە گریان
وێنەیەک
پڕ پڕ بێ لە بۆنی شەهید
پڕ پڕ بێ لە ڕەنگی بارین
پڕ پڕ بێ لە نیگا
وێنەیەک پڕ پڕ بێ
لە نمەی بەخێرهاتنەوە و
پڕ پڕ بێ لە گمەی خواحافیزیی و
پڕ پڕ بێ لە دوعا
وێنەیەک
پڕ پڕ بێ لە لێزمەی هەنسک و
پڕ پڕ بێ لە هاژەی چاکوچۆنی
پڕ پڕ بێ لە لەرەی دەنگی منااڵنی
نێرگزفرۆش و
پڕ پڕ بێ لە سابونکەران و
لە پیرەمێرد و
پڕ پڕ بێ لە بۆنی خۆشی
ڕۆژنامەی ژین
وێنەیەک
پڕ پڕ بێ لە گمە و
پڕ پڕ بێ لە فڕین و
پڕ پڕ بێ لە تریقانەوەی برین!
وێنەیەک
پڕ پڕ بێ لە شەوی نووسینی
یەکەمین نامەی عیشق و
پڕ پڕ بێ لە ڕاڕایی و
پڕ پڕ بێ
لە کوژانەوە و
لە مسۆدە و
پڕ پڕ بێ لە دەسخەتی ناخۆش و
پڕ پڕ بێ لە دەسخەتی جوان

of calamity
full of the neighbourhood children
a picture
full of complaints
of pain
a picture
full of hugs
of falling down
of kisses and
of tears
a picture
full of the smell of martyrs
and the colours of raining
full of gazes
a picture full of
the drizzle of welcomes and
full of the cooing of farewell and
full of prayers
a picture
full of the downpour of sobs and
the cascade of greeting
full of the frequencies of the voices of children
who sell daffodils and
full of the Saboonkaran neighbourhood and
of the poet Piramerd and
full of the lovely fragrance of
Zheen newspaper
a picture
full of cooing and
flight and
full of the guffaws of wounds!
A picture
full of the night of writing
the first love letter and
full of anxiety and
full
of erasing and
of draft notes and
full of ugly handwriting and
of beautiful handwriting

وێنەیەک

پڕ پڕ بێ لە بێکەس و

پڕ پڕ بێ لە داری ئازادی و

پڕ پڕ بێ

لە بیست و حەوت هەزار چەمۆڵە و

لە بیست و حەوت هەزار

دڵۆپە ڕەنج و

لە بیست و حەوت هەزار

باخچەی چۆڵ

وێنەیەک

پڕ پڕ بێ لە بادی خۆشمرورەکەی

نالی و

پڕ پڕ بێ لە حەبیبە و

پڕ پڕ بێ لە عیشقی خاک و خۆڵ

وێنەیەک

پڕ پڕ بێ لە تەسلیمکردنەوەی حەق

پڕ پڕ بێ لە مەرەخەسکردنی گورگ

پڕ پڕ بێ

لە ماچکردنی ئەملاولای ڕێوی

پڕ پڕ بێ لە بۆنی تاریکیی و

پڕ پڕ بێ لە دەنگی باران

وێنەیەک

پڕ پڕ بێ لە شیعری حاجی و

لە چڵەخورماکەی گیونای

پڕ پڕ بێ لە بێشکچیی و

لە عەلەوی

پڕ پڕ بێ لە هەجووە مزرەکانی

شێخ و

لە بۆنی پەمەیی ئازادیی و

پڕ پڕ بێ لە ڕەنگی شیرینی ژیان!

دەستتم بدەرێ ... خێرا کە

وێنەیەکی بەکۆمەڵمان بگرە

تا تەواو تەواو

لە یەکتر بزر نەبووین

دەستتم بدەرێ خێراکە

وێنەیەکی بەکۆمەڵمان بگرە

تا نەبووین بەژێر دەست و پێی چەقۆوە

تا دایکم لە من

a picture
full of the poet Fayaq Bekas and
full of his Tree of Freedom and
full
of twenty-seven thousand scornful and
of twenty-seven thousand
drops of suffering and
of twenty-seven thousand
deserted gardens
a picture
full of the poet Nali's
Joyful Wind and
full of his lover and
full of love for Khakukhol village
a picture
full of surrendering the truth
full of releasing wolves
full
of kissing both cheeks of the fox
full of the smell of darkness and
full of the sound of the rain
a picture
full of Haji Qadir Koyi's poetry and
of Yılmaz Güney's Palme d'Or
full of İsmail Beşikçi and
of Alavı
full of the tart lampoons
of Sheikh Reza Talabani and
of the pink scent of freedom and
full of the sweet colours of life!
Give me your hands… hurry up
take a group picture of us
before we get lost
to each other completely
give me your hands, hurry up
take a group picture of us
before the knife waylays us
before my mother is lost to me

من له منالیی
منالیی له کۆڵان
یهک لهویتر
ههموومان له ههموومان
بزر نهبووین
دهستتم بدهرێ خێراکه
وێنهیهکی تهنیاییمان بگره
دهشێ
یهکتر نهبینینهوه ئیتر
وێنهیهک
که پشتمان له ڕیزێ چۆڵهوانی و
ئهوبهرمان کۆڵانێ دووری و
به زهردهخهنهوه
دهستمان کردبێته ملی یهکتر
خێراکه ههستهوه
وێنهیهکمان بگره
تا تهواو تهواو
لهیهکتر بزر نهبووین!

سلێمانی شوباتی ٩٩٩١

ئهو گونده

لهو گونده، هونهر و میدیتاسیۆن یهک دهگرن. هونهری وشهی ساده و ڕۆژانه که
وهستایانه بهکار هێنراون بۆ کێشانی وێنهی کهسانیک که لهو گوندهدا وهک "زین
ماستهر" دهژین. ئهوان تهواو ئاگاداری کۆنسێپتهکانی ژیان، بهڵام لهگهڵ سروشتی
خۆرسکی ژینگهکهیاندا سازاندوویان. ئهوان بهشداریی ههڵبژاردنهکان دهکهن،
بهڵام تهنیا دهنگ به باڵنده لیبراڵهکان دهدهن. یاسا ئاڵۆزهکانی ماتماتیک شارهزا
نین، بهڵام به ههناسه یادی شکۆفهی گوڵ دهژمێرن. له ههر بهندێکی ئهم شیعرهدا،
سادهیی بهرانبهر به گهردشیکی ئاڵۆزی رۆحانی ئاوێتهیه.

بۆ تابلۆی «پێکهنین»ی هونهرمهند جهزا بهکر

لهو گونده
خۆر له خۆرهههڵاتهوه ههڵدێ و
له خۆرئاواوه ئاوا دهبێ
لهو گونده
قهدهر پیاوێکه گهنمرهنگ

I am from childhood
childhood from neighbourhood
one from the other
all of us from all of us
give me your hands, hurry up
take a picture of our solitude
perhaps
we'll not see each other again
a picture
with our backs to a row of desert and
facing a neighbourhood of distance and
with a smile
with our arms around each other's necks
hurry up, get up again
take a picture of us
before we are lost
to each other
completely!

Slemani, February, 1999

THAT VILLAGE

In this village, art and meditation come together. The artfully simple everyday words are used to evoke images of people who live like zen masters. They are fully aware of worldly concepts, but have chosen to adapt them to their indigenous ways. They do participate in elections, but only to vote for liberal birds. They don't know of mathematical concepts, but they do count in their breath the anniversary of flower blossoms. Simplicity is contradicted by complex spiritual cycles which appear in each stanza of the poem.

for 'Laughter', a painting by Jaza Bakr

In that village
the sun rises in the east and
sets in the west
in that village
destiny is a swarthy man

نیوەڕوان بە فیکە لێدانەوە
بەژێر سێبەری دارهەنارەکاندا
ڕەت دەبێ
لەو گوندە
لە هەر جێگاپێیەکدا قسەیەک ڕوواوە
لەسەر پەلکی هەر درەختێ
چرای جریوەیەک هەلکراوە
خەلکی ئەو گوندە
نە گوێ لە هەواڵەکان دەگرن و
نە لاپەڕەی یەکەمی ڕۆژنامەکان دەخوێننەوە
کەچی لە هەلبژاردندا
دەنگ بۆ کوکووختییە لیبراڵەکان دەدەن
خەلکی ئەو گوندە
هیچ لە لێکدان و دابەشکردن و لێدەرکردن نازانن
کەچی بە هەناسە
ساڵڕۆژی پشکوتنی گوڵە قەرسیلییەکان
حیساب دەکەن
بە بۆن ... بە پیر دیداری گوڵئەستێرەوە دەچن
خەلکی ئەو گوندە
کە دەبنە میوانی گەردەلوول
وردو درشت
گیرفانەکانیان پڕ دەکەن لە سێبەر و هەور و
هەتاو
کەچی لەو سەرەوە
بە باوەشی ئەستێرەوە دێنەوە
خەلکی ئەو گوندە
بە سڵاو خۆیان دەکەن بە ماڵدا و
بە سڵاو لەماڵ دەچنە دەر

لەو گوندە
شەوانە ئەستێرەکان دەبنە ئاو
دەتکێنە زاری نوقڵینی پێکەنینەوە

لەو گوندە
شنەبا کۆچەرەکان
لە ئامێزی تریفەدا خۆیان دەکوژن
لە ئامێزی بارێزەدا
هەناسە دەدەن و دەڕوێن و
سەوز دەبن

who passes at noon whistling
beneath the shade of the pomegranate trees
in that village
a word has sprouted at every footprint
the lantern of cooing has been switched on
in the branches of every tree
the people of that village
don't listen to the news
nor do they read the newspapers's front page
but in the elections
they vote for liberal doves
the people of that village
know nothing about multiplication, division and subtraction
but they count
the anniversary of the blooming of the barley
like breathing
they go to meet fireflies
by smell
the people of that village
when they become guests of the whirlwind
both the young and the old
fill their pockets with shadows,
clouds and sunlight
but from there
they return in the arms of the stars
the people of that village
enter and leave home
exchanging greetings

In that village
the stars melt at night
and drip into laughter's sweet little candy mouth

In that village
the migratory breezes
commit suicide in the moonlight's arms
breath, sprout and grow
in the rainstorm's embrace

لەو گوندە
گوناه پێی شورەیی نییە
ڕووت و قووت بەدوای ئارەزوودا ڕاکا
کەچی حەقیقەت پێی شەرمە
لە کونی دەرگاوە تەماشای
خۆ ڕووت کردنەوەی گومان کا
کەچی تینوێتیی پێی شەرمە
گوێ بۆ چرپەی تەروبری خۆشەویستیی
هەڵبخا

لەو گوندە
ماسییەکان هەر لە یەکەمین بینینەوە
عاشقی قولایی دەبن
لەوسەرەوە لەسەر نووکی پێ
بە هێڵە خەتەرناک و خۆشەکانی
خنکان و تەنگەنەفەسبووندا دێنەوە

لەو گوندە
کەس تاقیبی فڕینی پاسارییەکان ناکا
بۆ نموونە:
هیچ کانییەک بە شیعرێ نالێ
ئەمڕۆ لەکوێ بووی؟

لەو گوندە
باغەوانێ دەناسم
سیمای لە هەور و
دەستەکانیشی لە گزنگ
کە دەنوێ:
پەمەیی ... پەمەیی دەچێتەوە
کە دەڕوا:
درەخت و پەپوولە و شیعری
ئەو دونیایەی دێنە سەیر

لەو گوندە
بوومەتە هاوڕێی ئاوێنەیەک
عومرێکە
خۆی لە زەریادا تەماشا دەکا!

سلێمانی، ١٩٩٣

36

In that village
sin is not to be ashamed of
running nakedly after desire
but the truth is something else to be ashamed of
looking at doubt's striptease
through the keyhole
but thirst is to be ashamed of
listening to love's amorous whispers

In that village
the fish from the first sight
fall in love with depth
then return, on tiptoe,
along the dangerous and beautiful lines
of drowning and choking

In that village
no one observes the sparrows' flight
for instance,
no spring asks a poem,
"Where were you today?"

In that village
I know a gardener
whose appearance is of the clouds and
his hands of daybreak
when he sleeps;
he turns pink, so pink
when he walks;
trees, butterflies and the poetry
of the world come to see him

In that village
I have become friends with a mirror
which looks at itself in the sea
for a lifetime!

Slemani, 1993

له چاوتروکانێکدا سەری ولاتم سپی بوو

ئەم شیعره ویرانکارییەکانی هەلەبجه له کیمیابیبارانەکەی مانگی ئازاری سالی
١٩٨٨وەبیر دەهینینتەوه. شتێکی نائاسایی روو دەدات. سال دەبیته پینج وەرز، شەو
و روژ دەبنه بیستوپینج کاتژمیر، خۆر له خۆرئاواوه هەلدیت و له خۆرهەلاتەوه
ئاوا دەبیت، له چاتروکانێکدا تەمی سپیی مردن شاریک دادەپۆشیت. لەو کپی
و بیدەنگییه چرەدا، به حال دەنگێکی گریاناوی له دوورەوه دیت. ئەوه دەنگی
کەس نییه جگه له دەنگی شیعر که به نوینەرایەتی خودا بۆ سەرەخۆشی و داوای
لیبووردن هاتووه.

بۆ زامه سارپیژنەبووەکانی هەلەبجه

ئەو ئیوارەیه
میلی کاتژمیر بیستوپینج جار
بەنیو شپرزەیی روحی ئەودا فری
سال بووه پینج وەرز
بەهار، هاوین، پاییز، هەلەبجه، زستان
خۆر سەری ئاوابوونی لێ هاتەوه یەک
له چاتروکانێکدا سەری ولاتم سپیی بوو!

ئەی تاسەی تەروبری یەکەمین ویسال
ئەی قاسیدی به ویقاری سەرەتا
خۆت لەوێ بووی
که بادی خۆشمرور هەلی کرد و
ئەو سیروانی سیاچەمانەیەمی
بۆ هیجرەتی دیاری غەریبیی هەلیچچا
به بالی هەنگاوت هەلمگره ئەی پەیکی شارەزا
توند توند له مەوجی تەروبری روانینتم بیێچچه
تا لەسەر لەپی ئیشتیاقت سەوز بم
هەلمگره ئەی بادی سەبا
لەسەر لەرەی دەنگت
تا له شوینپیی سەرابیی هیجرەتتا
بال بگرم
هیجرەته .. هیجرەت ... هیجرەت
هیجرەتی شار و شیعر و شنروی
هیجرەتی هەلەبجه
ئەوەتاین بمانبه
لەسەر شابالی هیجرەتت هەلمانگره
هیند هاتوینەوه یەک
له جانتای مەکتەبی مندالیکدا
جیی هەموومان دەبیتەوه

38

IN THE BLINK OF AN EYE, MY COUNTRY'S HAIR TURNED WHITE

The poem remembers the devastation of Halabja in a chemical attack in March 1988. Something unusual happens: the year a fifth season is added, night and each day becomes 25 hours, the sun rises from west and sets in the east; in a blink of an eye, a city is covered in a whitish fog of death. In that dense tranquillity, a faint cry is heard. It is the voice of none other than poetry who has come on behalf of God to send His condolences and ask forgiveness.

for the unhealed wounds of Halabja

That evening
the hour hand at twenty-five o'clock
flew through the bafflement of its soul
the year became five seasons
spring, summer, autumn, Halabja, winter
the sun got confused about when to set
In the blink of an eye, my country's hair turned white!

O the amorous desire of the first reunion
o the first dignified messenger
you were there from beginning
when the joyful wind blew and
pressured my Sirwan river of Siyachamana chanting
to migrate to the lands of exile
carry me on your winged feet, O you wise messenger
wrap me tightly in the moist waves of your gazes
till I sprout on the palms of your passion
carry me, O you West Wind
on the vibrations of your voice
till I take flight
in the footsteps of your migration's mirage
It's all migration… migration… migration
migration of the city, poetry and Shinrwe mountain
migration of Halabja
here we are, take us
carry us on the feathered pinions of your migration
we've shrunk so much
all of us can fit
in a child's school bag

ئێمە ئەمێستا خەمێکین ساڵخوردە
سپیی... سپیی دەچینەوە
ڕیز... ڕیز بەو ڕییەوە
دەڵێی بەفرین لە کاتی بارینا
دەڵێی چاوین لە کاتی ڕوانینا
دەڵێی باڵین لە کاتی فڕینا
دەڵێی پەلکە سەوزەکانی کانیئاشقانین
لەکاتی ژاکان و وەرینا!
بڕوانە ئەی پەیکی شارەزا
وڵاتم چنگێکی ماوەتەوە
بمانبە... سوودی نییە نامە
تەشریحی زەعیفی من و
غەمی ردێن سپیی هەڵەبجە نایەتە تەحریر
هەڵمانگرە نەرم... نەرم
لەسەر باڵی هاژەت
ڕیز... ڕیز لەگوڵدانی بەر پەنجەرەی
نەخۆشخانەکانی تاراندا بمانڕوێنە
توند توند لە خوڕەی جاریی فیراقمان بپێچە
تا لەسەر لەپی ئیشتیاقت سەوز بین

لەوێ بووی ئەی پەیکی شارەزا
ئەو ڕۆژەی جێکەڵبەی ژەهراویی گورگ
بە جەستەی کارئاسکەکەی
سەحرای هەڵەبجەمەوە بەجێما؟
لەوێ بوویت ... ئەو ڕۆژەی
گوڵان دڵی تێکەڵ هات و
سیروان لەپێ کەوت و
مێژوو ڕشایەوە؟
لەوێ بووی ئەی پەیکی شارەزا
ئەو بەهارەی نێرگز
چڵە چڵە سینگی خۆی دادڕی و
دیوان پەرە پەرە خۆی کوشت و
قەسیدە بەیت بەیت سەری هەڵگرت؟
لەوێ بووی ئەو ڕۆژەی
شاخ گریا و
کانی قوڵپ قوڵپ زریکاندی و
تڕێ هێشوو هێشوو وەری؟
تەنانەت تۆیش ئەی بادی خۆشمرور
فریای خوێندنەوەی ئەو چامە سەوزەی
هیجرەت نەکەوتی!
چنگێک هەناسە... ئەی بادی سەبا

40

we are an aged grief now
turning white, so white
row after row on that path
we look like snow pouring
we look like eyes staring
we look like wings flying
we look like the green branches of Kaniy Ashqan spring
withering and falling!
Look, O you wise messenger
a handful have left my country
take us… letters are pointless
to explain my weakness and
Halabja's grey-beard sorrow can't be written
carry us softly, so softly
on your rushing wings
row by row, plant us to sprout
in flower-pots on the window sills of Tehran hospitals
wrap us tightly, so tightly in the current of separation
till we sprout on the palms of your passion

Were you there, O you wise messenger,
the day when wolves' poisonous fang prints
were left on the fawn-body
of my Halabja's desert?
Were you there… the day
of Gulan village's nausea and
when Sirwan river could no longer walk and
history vomited?
Were you there, O you wise messenger
that Spring when daffodils
tore apart their chests stem by stem
and the divans committed suicide page by page
and the qasida left for exile verse after verse?
Were you there
the day mountains wept and
each bubble of spring water shrieked and
grapes fell cluster after cluster?
Even you, O joyful wind
did not get the chance to recite
the green ballad of migration!
A handful of breaths… O you West Wind

بۆ هەنگ ... بۆ هەڵەبجە ... بۆ هێزۆ
تۆزێک جریوە ئەی بادی سەبا
بۆ گەڵا .. بۆ گوڵ .. بۆ گروگاڵ
هێندەی سەرەدەرزییەک نیگا
ئەی بادی سەبا
بۆ هیجرەتی ناوەختی ئاوێنە و چرا!!
لە جانتاکەتا جێمان بکەوە
توند توند لەسەر هەناسە و هەوا و هەور دامانخە
پەلک ... پەلک رواینمان
لە ئاسمان و زەوی و کتێبەکان هەلکێشە
تەل تەل رەنگمان
لە گۆرانی و حەکایەت و تابلۆکان بکەوە
ئێمە قەبیلەیەکی گوناە بووین .. گوناە
بە زیندووویی مۆمیاکراین
باڵەکانمان کرا بە باوەشین
چاومان کرا بە مۆروو
پەنجەکانمان کرا بە تەسبیح
دڵمان کرا بە گوڵدان
بمانبە لەسەر باڵی هەناسەت ئەی بادی سەبا

بە مۆزەخانەی دڵ و چاو و قامکی مندالیی خۆماندا
بمانگێرە
بمانبەرەوە بۆ ئەوێ
بۆ لای ماڵە باجێنەکان
بۆ لای بووکەشووشە بێدەنگەکان
بمانبەرەوە بۆ ناو وێنە رەش و سپییەکان
بۆ ژێر درەختەکانی کانیئاشقان
بمانبەرەوە بۆ لای سەفەرەکان
بۆ لای عیشق و خەون و کتێبەکان
بمانبەرەوە بۆ پاڵ ئاگردانەکان
بۆ سەرەتای روان
ئەوەتاین:
پۆل ... پۆل بمانبەرەوە بۆ ئەوێ
سپیی سپیی دەچینەوە
وەک هەڵەبجەی ناو گۆرانییەکان
وەک هەڵەبجەی رەشداگەرراو و قژ بڕی
بەردەم مەغازە و تەرمینال و نەخۆشخانەکان
سپیی سپیی دەچینەوە
ئەی بادی سەبا
وەک هەڵەبجەی پێکراو و جیهێلراوی

42

For the bees... for Halabja... for hollyhocks
a few warbled notes, O you West Wind
for leaves... for flowers... for babbling
tiny as the eye of a needle
O you West Wind
for the untimely migration of mirrors and lanterns!
Make room for us in your bag
spread us tight, so tight on breath, air and clouds
draw up our gaze leaf by leaf
in the sky, the earth and the books
remove our roots strand by strand
from songs, tales and paintings
we were a poor tribe, so poor
we were mummified alive
our wings were turned into a hand fan
our eyes into beads
our fingers into rosaries
our hearts were turned into flower-pots
take us on the wings of your breath, O you West Wind

Take us on a tour of
the museum of our childhood's hearts, eyes and fingers
take us back there
to the dollshouses
to the silent dolls
take us back into the black-and-white photographs
to beneath the trees of the Kaniy Ashqan
take us back to the journeys
towards love, dreams and books
take us back to the fireplaces
to the very origins of sprouting
here we are:
Take us back there flock by flock
we turn white, so white
like Halabja in the songs
like blackened Halabja with its ragged hair
in front of shops, bus terminals and hospitals
we turn white, so white
O you West Wind
like wounded and abandoned Halabja

ناو گۆڕەپانی جەنگەکان
وەک هەڵەبجەی دەست و پەنجە لەگۆکەوتووی
بەر ویستگەکانی چاوەڕوانیی
وەک هەڵەبجەی تاک و تەنیا و ژەهرزەدەی
سەر کورسیی چاخانەکان
وەک هەڵەبجەی ناو زەمەنی نوتقی سارد
شەڕی سارد ... گۆرانی سارد ... عەشقی سارد
وەرزی سارد
وەک هەڵەبجەی
ناو دۆسیەی تۆز لێنیشتووی
ئەمینستی ئینتەرناشناڵ و ئەنجومەنی ئاسایش و یوئێن
سپیی سپیی دەچینەوە ئەی بادی سەبا
تەماشا
دەڵێی بەفرین لەکاتی بارینا
دەڵێی چاوین لەکاتی ڕوانینا
دەڵێی باڵین لەکاتی فڕینا
دەڵێی پەلکە سەوزەکانی کانیئاشقانین
لەکاتی ژاکان و وەرینا!

سلێمانی سەرەتای ١٩٩٥

on the battlefields
like Halabja with its numb fingers
in front of the waiting stations
like the lonely and poisoned Halabja
on the chairs of the teahouses
like Halabja in the era of cold speech,
cold war… cold songs… cold love
cold seasons
like Halabja
in the dusty files of
Amnesty International, the Security Council and the UN
we turn white, so white, O you West Wind
look
we look like snow pouring
we look like eyes staring
we look like wings flying
we look like the green branches of Kaniy Ashqan
withering and falling!

Slemani, early 1995

BIOGRAPHICAL NOTES

DILAWAR KARADAGHI is a Kurdish poet, translator, essayist, playwright and theatre director. Born in the city of Slemani in southern Kurdistan in 1963, he graduated in drama at the Baghdad University College of Fine Arts in 1986. After the Iraq-Iran war, he went into exile in Iran for two years, moving to Sweden in 1999. Dilawar is one of the most important contemporary Kurdish poets, having published ten collections of poems. He has been nominated for major poetry awards, including the 2019 American Pushcart Prize. His poetry was translated into Arabic and published in Syria in 2000, receiving a great deal of attention in the Arabic-speaking world. Readings of his poetry have been held in Kurdistan, the UK, Sweden and Iran and his work has been translated into English, French, Swedish, Arabic, Persian and Spanish.

Jiyar Homer is a translator and editor from Kurdistan, a member of Kashkul, the Center for Arts and Culture at the American University of Iraq, Sulaimani (AUIS), and an editor at Îlyan magazine and the Balinde Poetry publishing house. He speaks Kurdish, English, Spanish, Portuguese, Arabic, and Persian. He specialises in translating Latin American literature into Kurdish and Kurdish literature into various languages, bringing over 100 authors into publication in more than 30 countries. His full-length translations include works by Juan Carlos Onetti, Carlos Ruiz Zafón, Bachtyar Ali, Farhad Pirbal and Sherzad Hassan. One of his translations into English appeared in *The Best Literary Translations Anthology 2024*. Additionally, he is a member of Kurdish PEN.

MIKE BAYNHAM is a translator and poet from West Yorkshire. In retirement he has returned to an early love of poetry translation, translating mainly from Spanish, Arabic and occasionally from Persian. His translations have been published in a number of publications, including *Artrage, Las Flechas de Artemis, Transference*. He has collaborated with the Moroccan zejal poet Adil Latefi and with the Kurdish Syrian poet, Ceger Hillo. He was awarded 2nd Prize in the 2023 Stephen Spender Prize for his translation of a poem by Adil Latefi, and received a Commendation in the 2022 Stephen Spender Prize for his translation of a poem by Sohrab Sepehri.